THE WORLD'S BEST PUZZLES

Charles Barry Townsend

Sterling Publishing Co., Inc.   New York

DEDICATION

To my wife, Maryann,
whose love, encouragement,
and patience have made
my books possible.

Library of Congress Cataloging-in-Publication Data

Townsend, Charles Barry.
  The world's best puzzles.

  Includes index.
  Summary: Approximately 100 puzzles dealing with
mathematics, dexterity, words, games, geometry, and
logic, which have perplexed and entertained puzzlers
over the past century.
  1. Puzzles—Juvenile literature. [1. Puzzles]
I. Title.
GV1493.T685 1986   793.73   85-30284

Published by Sterling Publishing Company, Inc.
387 Park Avenue South, New York, N.Y. 10016
© 1986 by Charles Barry Townsend
Distributed in Canada by Sterling Publishing
% Canadian Manda Group, P.O. Box 920, Station U
Toronto, Ontario, Canada M8Z 5P9
Distributed in Great Britain and Europe by Cassell PLC
Villiers House, 41/47 Strand, London WC2N 5JE, England
Distributed in Australia by Capricorn Link Ltd.
P.O. Box 665, Lane Cove, NSW 2066
Manufactured in the United States of America
All rights reserved

Sterling ISBN 0-8069-4734-9

Contents

Introduction

One of the main questions that I have been asked concerning this book is, "How did you go about selecting the world's best puzzles?" Well, first off, let me state that my list of what constitutes the best puzzles in the world would be different from a list that you might put together, and your list would certainly be different from one that Martin Gardner would compile. It's strictly an editorial "feel" on the writer's part. However, one thing that you definitely need is a good library, one that covers the field of puzzles over the past century. Happily, being a "pack rat" where puzzle books are concerned, I've amassed just such a library. It's been my main source of inspiration when writing my puzzle and game books.

Some of the puzzles presented here were selected because they have withstood the test of time. They can be found repeatedly in puzzle books from the 1890s to the 1980s. Some, like the "Find-the-Wife" brain teaser on page 72, are strictly one-of-a-kind problems; others, like the "Sugar" puzzle on page 30, rely on a "surprise" solution for solving what, at first glance, appears to be an impossible problem.

To provide the maximum interest for the reader, I have tried to generate the greatest variety of problems. As many areas of puzzledom as possible have been covered. You'll find problems dealing with mathematics, dexterity, words, games, geometry, and logic. There are puzzles employing coins, cards, matchsticks, pencils, books, glasses, toothpicks, rope, string, ice, paper, water, money, checkers, sugar, a yardstick, dice, and many other items.

In short, every puzzle has been selected for both its uniqueness, and for the time-tested quality of its content. In this volume, you will find 102 of the best-loved problems that have perplexed and entertained puzzlers over the past century. Give them all a good try, and when you're finished try stumping your friends with them. Enough said. It's now time to put on your thinking caps and get down to work. On your mark! Get set! Start puzzling!

Charles Barry Townsend

The World's Best Puzzlers (?): Author Charles Barry Townsend and his sons Mark (left) and Chris (right).

PUZZLES

The World's Best "Farm" Puzzle

Many years ago a farmer, named Hiram, had a square field. He sold one quarter of his land (the shaded area) to buy farm equipment. When the farmer grew older, he decided to divide what was left of his farm into four parcels of land, each exactly the same shape and size. Each parcel was to contain three square acres. Can you figure out how Hiram accomplished this feat?

The World's Best "Bully" Puzzle

The next time somebody tries to push you around, tell him that you don't think he's so tough and that you can make him powerless to hit you if you so choose. Remove a handkerchief from your pocket, and inform him that: 1, you will place the handkerchief on the floor; 2, he must stand on one edge of it; and 3, you will stand on the opposite edge. Notwithstanding the fact that you are only inches apart, you will inhibit him, through the use of your superior abilities, from laying the proverbial finger on you.

Now that you've heard the plot behind the wager, how do you think you are going to escape getting bopped in the beezer?

The World's Best "Monument" Puzzle

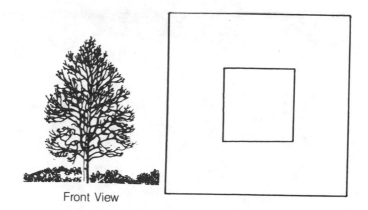

Front View

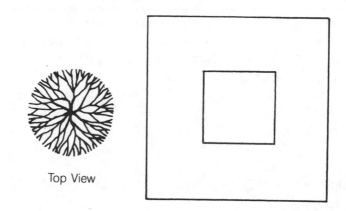

Top View

Here is a giant monument dedicated to puzzler solvers everywhere. The funny thing about this monument is that when viewed from the front it looks exactly the same as when seen from directly above. Do you know what this monument looks like when viewed from the side?

The World's Best "Window" Puzzle

Shown here is a store window that measures 7 feet high by 7 feet wide. The store decorator wants to paint half the window blue and still have a square, clear section of window that measures 7 feet high by 7 feet wide. How would he do this?

The World's Best "Soda Straw" Puzzle

Now here's a problem that will tax your skills. You must lift an empty soda bottle off a table using only one hand and a straw. There are two rules that must be followed: You cannot tie the straw into a knot, and the straw is not allowed to touch any part of the outside of the bottle.

The World's Best "Fish Tank" Puzzle

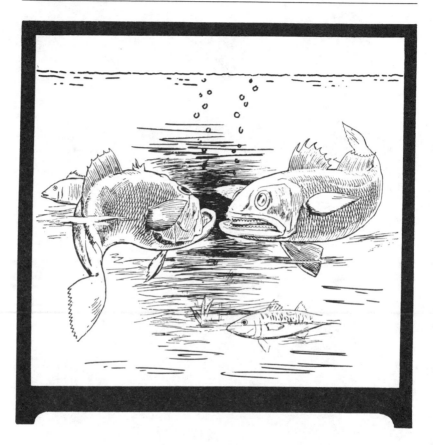

The fish tank shown here is almost filled to the top with water. Without using a measuring cup of any kind, or a measuring stick, can you remove enough water from the tank so that the water level will be exactly in the middle of the tank? The solution is easier than you think! *Note*: This can also be tried with a glass of water, which will be much less sloppy then a fish tank.

The World's Best "Coin" Puzzle

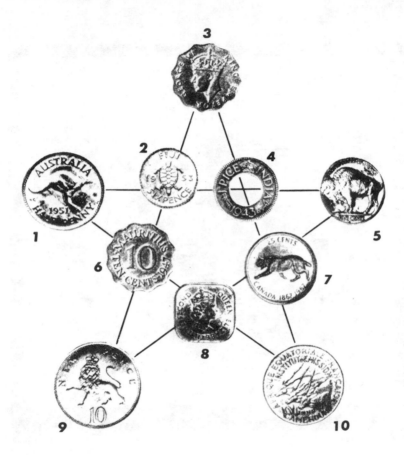

Here's a valuable puzzle for you to solve. Place nine coins on the star, one on each of the world coins except coin number eight. The object of this puzzle is to remove all but one of the coins from the star. You remove a coin by jumping another coin over it along one of the lines. The position that you jump to, beyond the coin, must be empty (the moves are the same as those you would make in a game of checkers).

If you can solve this puzzle within 15 minutes, consider yourself rich in ability.

The World's Best "Matchstick" Puzzle

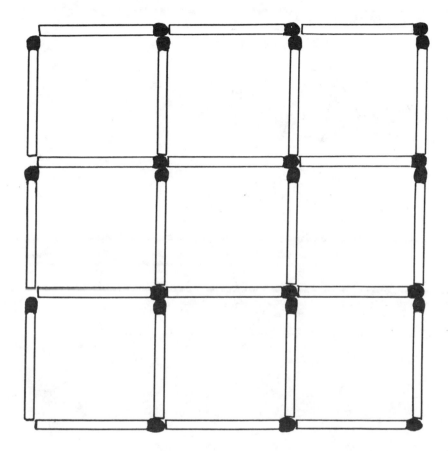

This is truly a matchless puzzle. Arrange 24 matchsticks as shown. The pattern forms nine squares. The puzzle is to remove eight of these matchsticks in such a way as to leave only two squares.

The World's Best "Line" Puzzle

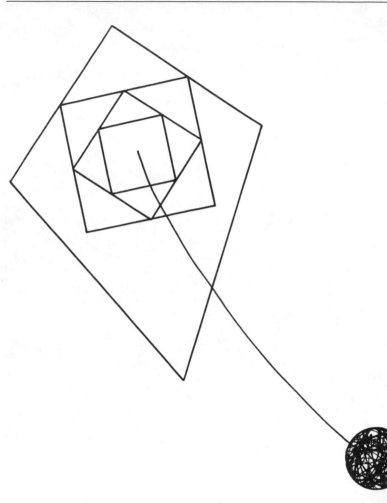

Shown is the famous "Puzzle Kite." To solve the puzzle, you must draw the kite, and the string attached to it, using one continuous line. The line cannot cross itself at any point, nor can you go over any part of the line more than once. You must start the line at the ball of string and end it in the middle of the kite.

The World's Best "Book" Puzzle

Here is a puzzle that will really perplex your friends. Tie a piece of string around the middle of a fairly heavy book, say two or three pounds. Then fasten one end of the string to a doorknob so that the book hangs about a foot down from it. Taking hold of the string below the book, tell your friends that you can pull the string and make it break either above or below the book at will. They will be astonished to discover that this can be done. Do you know how this wonderful feat of magic is accomplished?

The World's Best "Ice-Cream-Stick" Puzzle

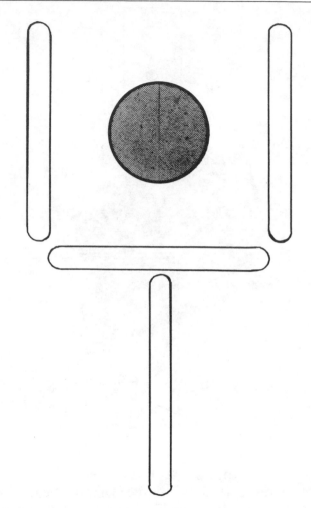

Let's pretend that the four ice-cream sticks shown represent a tall, stemmed glass, and the colored circle is a large, juicy cherry. You must remove the cherry from the glass by moving two of the sticks to new positions. You cannot move the cherry, and you must retain the exact shape of the glass.

The World's Best "Pizza" Puzzle

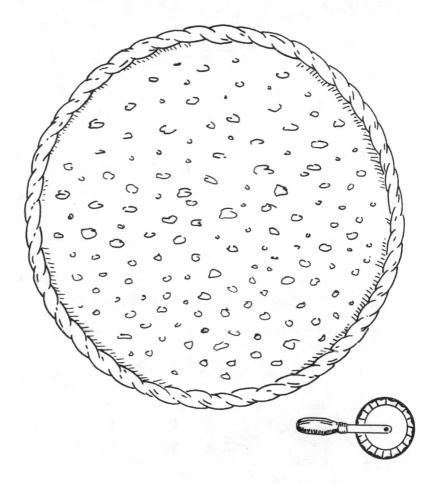

This is a very tasty puzzle. You must divide this pizza into eight equal pieces using only three cuts with the pizza cutter. All of the cuts must be in a straight line.

The World's Best "Counting" Puzzle

Professor Pepper's little "Problem-Generating" toy has once again created a puzzle masterpiece! The geometric figure shown here is made up of many triangles of different sizes. Can you count the exact number of triangles? *Hint:* There are more than 30 triangles in the picture.

The World's Best "Toothpick" Puzzle

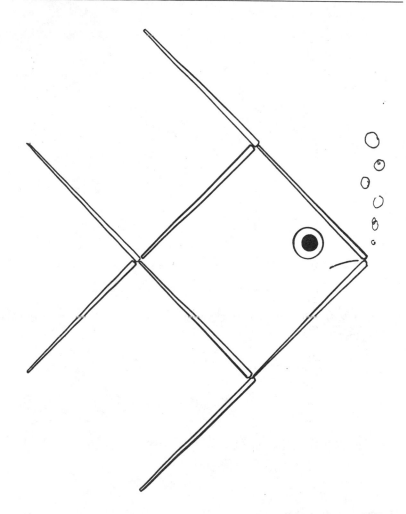

Arrange eight toothpicks as shown. Place a button in the square for an eye.

Suddenly our Toothpick Tuna sees a shark! He must turn around and swim for his life. Can you move three of the toothpicks, and the button, to new locations so that our fish will be swimming away to the left?

The World's Best "Rope" Puzzle

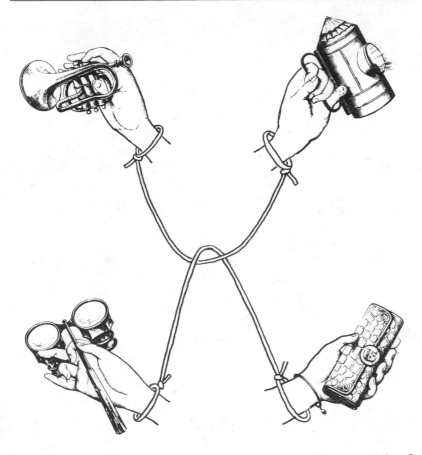

Try this puzzle with a friend. Loosely tie a short length of rope to both of your wrists. Have your friend do the same with another piece of rope that has been looped over the first rope. When this has been accomplished you will both be securely joined as shown above.

Your problem is to separate yourself from your friend without untying the knots, cutting the ropes, or slipping your hands out of the loops. It's easier then it looks!

Note: The objects featured in this illustration are from the turn of the century. Note in particular the flashlight on the upper right and the opera glasses on the lower left.

The World's Best "Stamp" Puzzle

Here's a neat "Stamp Stumper." Shown are six stamps from around the world. Our problem is to arrange these stamps in the form of a cross. However, there must be four stamps in each line of the cross. *Hint*: One stamp can be in both lines of the cross.

The World's Best "Ice Cube" Puzzle

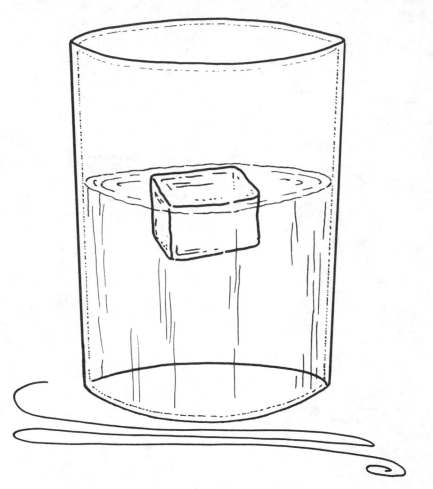

Here's an interesting scientific problem. Drop a small ice cube into a partially filled glass of water. Next, get a foot-long piece of thread or string. The puzzle is to remove the ice cube from the glass using only the string as a lifting device. You cannot tie a loop in the string, and you cannot touch the ice cube with your fingers. *Hint*: You'll really be worth your salt if you can solve this mystery!

The World's Best "Spelling" Puzzle

1. NODPAL

2. DSNCAOLT

3. RILBAUGA

4. ELANP

5. GLEDANN

6. UANMARI

7. SATNKPIA

All right students, take your seats for the "Spelling Bee." Perhaps I should say "Arranging Bee." Listed are the names of seven countries of the world. For the test, I have scrambled the letters that make up each name. It's up to you to rearrange them correctly. Five out of seven will get you a passing grade.

The World's Best "Train" Puzzle

Out West, there's a single-track railroad that goes through Old Baldy Mountain. Inside the mountain, the tunnel is only wide enough for one train. At exactly two o'clock one day, two trains entered the tunnel from opposite directions. Five minutes later each train came out of the opposite entrance to the tunnel. Neither train was damaged in any way. Now how on earth was this possible?

The World's Best "Paper" Puzzle

For this impossible puzzle we need a quarter, a dime, and a sheet of paper. Using the dime as a guide, draw a circle in the middle of the paper. Now, carefully cut this circle out of the paper. Your problem is now to push the quarter through the hole without tearing the paper. It can be done!

The World's Best "Hardware Shop" Puzzle

Shown here are four patrons of the New Old Bennington Hardware Shop. Within the past week all of them have moved into their own condominiums up the road in the Friar Briar Estates. The estates are made up of nine beautiful units overlooking Loon Lake. The customers have come to the hardware shop to buy something that the builder forgot to include with each unit. One will cost just $1.00. Eight will still only cost $1.00, but sixteen will cost $2.00. If they need one hundred and fifty, the total cost will be $3.00. Even if they order three hundred, they will still only pay $3.00. If this sounds confusing, believe me it isn't. For a total of $4.00, they each got what they came for and went away happy.

What were the items that these people purchased?

The World's Best "Dime" Puzzle

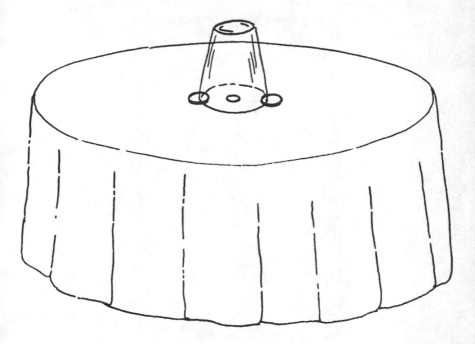

Here's another one of those "impossible" puzzles for you to solve. First, place a dime on top of a cloth-covered table. Next, place a quarter on either side of the dime. The quarters should be so placed that an inverted drinking glass will rest comfortably on the middle of each coin. After placing the glass on the coins, the setup should look like the one here. Now for the puzzle! You must remove the dime from under the glass without touching the glass or the quarters. Furthermore, you cannot slip anything under the glass in an effort to push the dime out. Impossible? Well . . .

The World's Best "Arrowhead" Puzzle

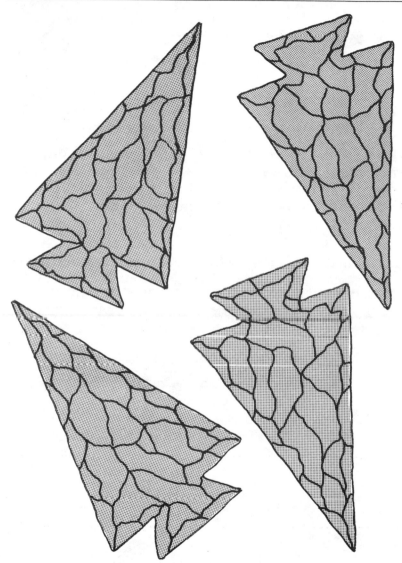

There is a way to turn these four Indian arrowheads into *five* arrowheads just by rearranging them. Let's see how good your aim is with this problem.

The World's Best "Yardstick" Puzzle

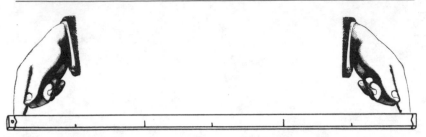

Here's a "Betcha" type of problem. Place the ends of a yardstick on your index fingers as illustrated. Now move your fingers towards one another. You will find that your fingers will always meet at the middle of the yardstick. It's impossible to make your fingers meet at any other spot.

If you reverse the action and try to move your fingers out from the middle to the ends of the ruler, you'll find that it can't be done. One finger will always stay at the middle of the stick, and the other will move out to the end.

Can you explain why these two actions take place as they do?

The World's Best "Paper Clip" Puzzle

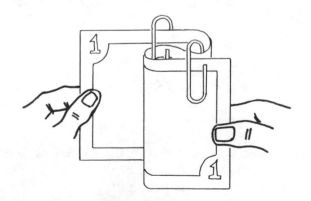

Challenge your friends that you can perform the famous "Linking Rings" trick. Take a dollar bill, fold it, and insert the paper clips in position as shown. State that without touching the two separated paper clips you will cause them to be linked together. Do you know how to do this?

The World's Best "Checkerboard" Puzzle

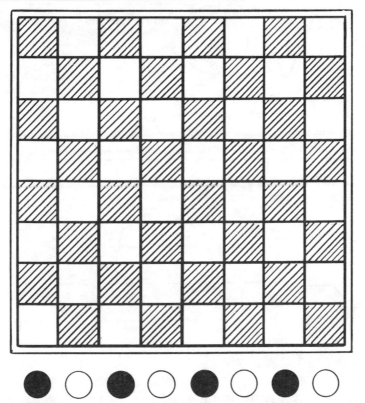

This puzzle's a real "classic." To set it up, you'll need a checkerboard and eight checkers of any color. Your problem is to place the eight checkers on the board so that no two shall be in the same line vertically, horizontally, or diagonally. This puzzle will keep you jumping.

The World's Best "Sugar" Puzzle

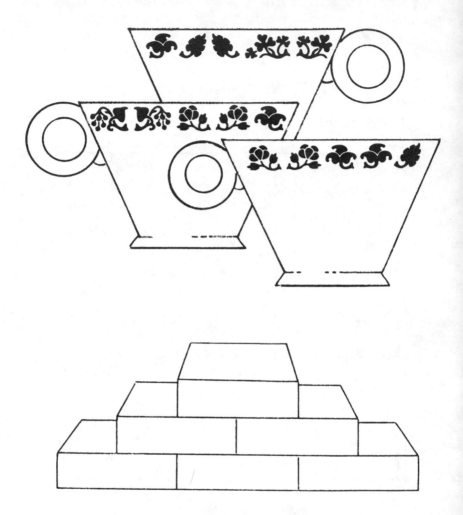

This is a sweet little problem to perplex your friends with. Place six lumps of sugar and three teacups on the table. What is required of the puzzle solver is to place the six lumps of sugar into the teacups in such a way that each cup will contain an odd number of lumps. All six lumps must be used, and none can be broken up in any way.

The World's Best "Dollar Bill" Puzzle

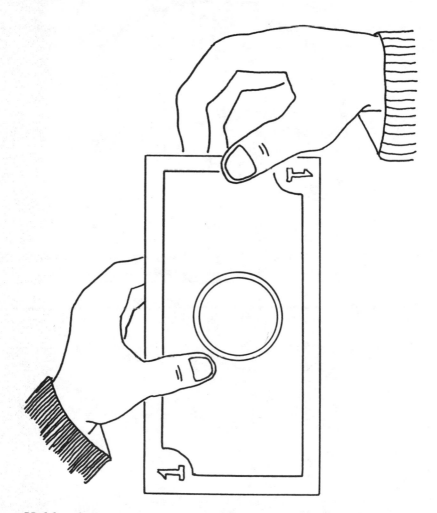

Hold a dollar bill in your right hand, at about chest level. Have someone place his left hand around the middle of the bill with the thumb and index finger about an inch apart. No part of his hand may touch the bill. Now, tell him that when you let go of the bill he won't be able to catch it before it passes through his fingers. It sounds easy, doesn't it?

The World's Best "Clock" Puzzle

Here's an interesting problem in time. Can you split this clockface into two equal halves so that the sum of the numbers on each half will be exactly the same? The pieces must be split along a straight line.

The World's Best "Money" Puzzle

The local bank is holding a contest, and if you're quick enough you might win first prize. The bank has a large jar that contains hundreds of coins. In fact, there is $700 in quarters, half-dollars, and silver dollars filling the bottle to the brim. There is the same number of each type of coin in the bottle. Can you determine how many of each there are?

The World's Best "Cannonball" Puzzle

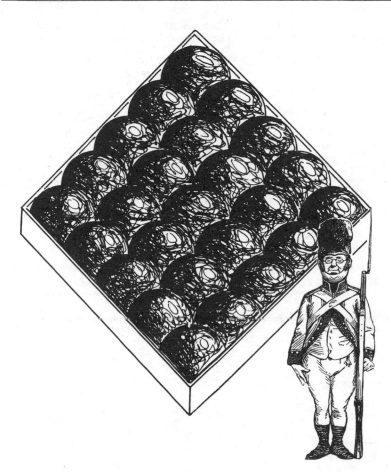

Many moons ago, Soldier Duncan was given the difficult job (?) of building a stack of cannonballs into the form of a pyramid in the middle of the Regimental Parade Grounds. After laying out the first row, Duncan ran out of cannonballs. He immediately sent out a hurried order for more and is shown here waiting for their delivery. Exactly how many more cannonballs will Duncan need to complete his pyramid?

The World's Best "Card" Puzzle

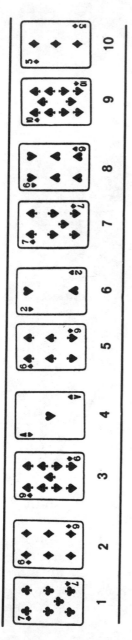

Lay out a row of ten cards on the table. Starting with any card, pick it up and move it left or right over the next two cards in the row and place it on top of the third card. You now have a pair. Next, pick up another single card and pass it left or right over the next two cards in the row (a pair counts as one card), and place it on the third single card. You now have another pair. Continue in this manner until you have five pairs upon the table.

34

The World's Best "Illusion" Puzzle

This is an outstanding optical illusion which appeared in a 1905 issue of *St. Nicholas* magazine. The article that came with it asks the reader to point out which of the three elephants and which of the three giraffes travelling through the long corridor in the picture is the tallest? Do you know the answer?

The World's Best "Bookworm" Puzzle

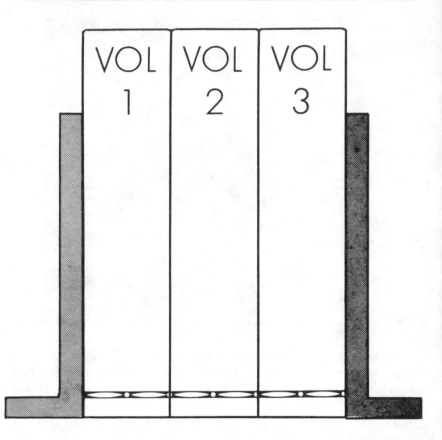

"The Case of the Ravenous Bookworm" is a great old puzzle. On top of the bookcase is a three-volume set of puzzle books. The front and back covers of the books are each 1/8 inch thick. The page section inside each book is exactly 2 inches thick. Now, if our bookworm starts eating at page one of volume 1 and eats, in a straight line, through to the last page of volume 3, how far will he travel?

The World's Best "Chess" Puzzle

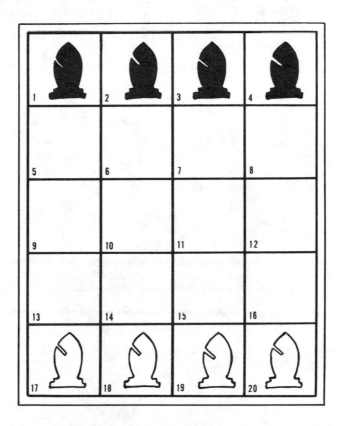

This "Bishop's" puzzle is played on a 4 by 5 square section of chessboard. Place four black bishops on squares 1 through 4 and four white bishops on squares 17 through 20. Your problem is to make the white bishops change places with the black bishops, using only bishop chess moves (they can move along diagonals only). Alternate play: first white, then black. No two pieces can be on the same square at any time, and no bishop may be left in a position where it could be taken by an opposing bishop. Also, you cannot take more then 36 moves to solve the puzzle.

The World's Best "Code" Puzzle

During World War I, two of Europe's top spies met at Kensington House in England, to exchange information. They were, of course, talking in code. Your assignment is to break this code in 15 minutes or less. Good luck. *Hint*: This code was created by rearranging the sequence of the letters in the alphabet. It is often referred to as "The Looking Glass Code."

The World's Best "Magic Square" Puzzle

The "Puzzle Computer" has done it again! Our program was supposed to create a Magic Square, using the numbers 1 through 9, that would add up to 15 in all directions. Instead, our cathode culprit came up with the answer shown. Can you solve this problem? Remember, the numbers must add up to 15 horizontally, vertically, and diagonally.

The World's Best "Geometry" Puzzle

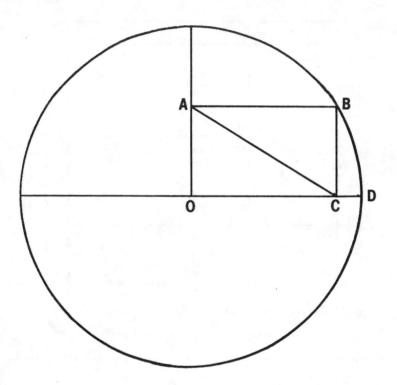

Here's a pretty geometric puzzle that's easier then it looks. The center of the circle is at O. The angle at AOC is 90 degrees. The line AB is parallel to the line OD. The segment OC is 5 inches long, and segment CD is 1 inch long. Your problem is to determine the length of line AC.

The World's Best "Starship" Puzzle

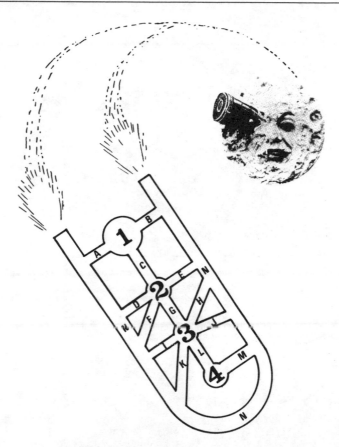

Starship 1 is heading back to Earth from the Moon. Shown here is the floor plan of the command deck of the forward module. Every hour Captain Birk makes his rounds. He has a route that will take him down every corridor that is labelled *A* through *M* once and only once. The outer corridor, *N*, can be entered any number of times. The four command centers (1, 2, 3, and 4) can also be entered any number of times. He always ends up his tour of inspection in command center 1. See if you can lay out the captain's route.

The World's Best "Archery" Puzzle

Friar Tuck has challenged Robin Hood to solve an ancient archery problem. He has to shoot six arrows into the target so that their combined scores will add up to exactly 100. Friar Tuck looks as if he knows the answer and can already taste the prize. *Hint*: Four of the arrows ended up in the same target circle.

The World's Best "Dice" Puzzle

This is a neat piece of "Puzzle Jugglery." Pick up a small paper cup in your right hand. Next, grip one die with your thumb and forefinger, and then balance a second die on top of it. The problem is to get both dice into the cup by tossing them in the air, one at a time, and catching them in the cup. Catching the first die is easy. However, when you try to catch the second one, the first die always seems to pop out of the cup. Give this puzzle a try before looking up the solution.

The World's Best "Button" Puzzle

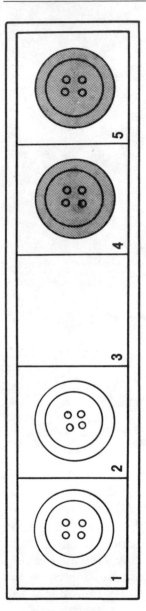

This is one of those delightful "substitution-type" puzzles. All you need are two white buttons, two red buttons, and this puzzle board. Place the buttons on the board as shown. Now, using only eight moves, you must cause these buttons to change places. The white buttons may only move to the right, and the red buttons may only move to the left. The buttons are moved by sliding them to the next empty space on the board. You can also jump one button over another button. However, the space beyond the button jumped must be empty.

The World's Best "Progression" Puzzle

1. O, T, T, F, F, ...
2. S, M, T, W, T, ...
3. D, N, O, S, A, ...

The new substitute teacher for today is Ms. Priscilla Sunshine, and does she have a test for you!

"Students, this is a progression test. You must add additional letters to each series of letters out to a point that indicates that you understand the meaning of the initials involved. Each letter, in each group, is the first letter of a word. Each group of letters has something in common. You have five minutes to solve this test. The winner gets to clean the erasers."

The World's Best "Chain" Puzzle

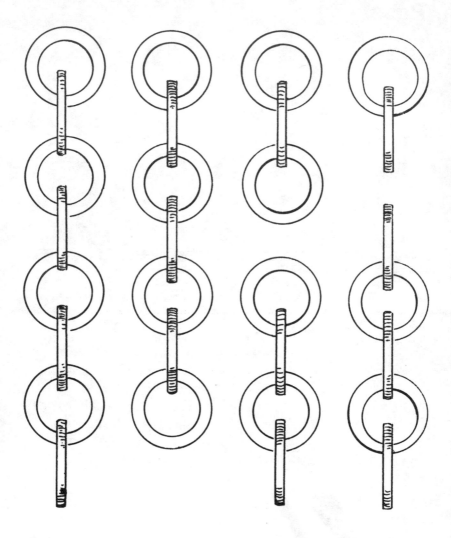

A man had six sections of chain that he wanted to join together to make one chain containing 29 links. He asked the blacksmith how much he would charge to do the job. The blacksmith told him that it would cost 50¢ to open a link and 75¢ to weld it shut. What was the cheapest price that the blacksmith could do the job for?

The World's Best "Footprint" Puzzle

Here's your chance to play detective. Can you figure out who, or what, made the tracks in the mud?

The World's Best "Word" Puzzle

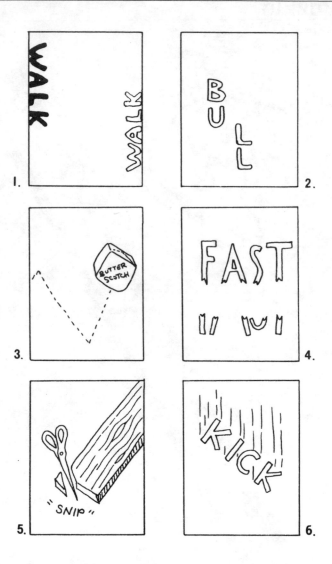

The six "word pictures" all stand for the names of some objects or expressions. They're tricky, but I bet that you can solve at least four of them.

The World's Best "Block" Puzzle

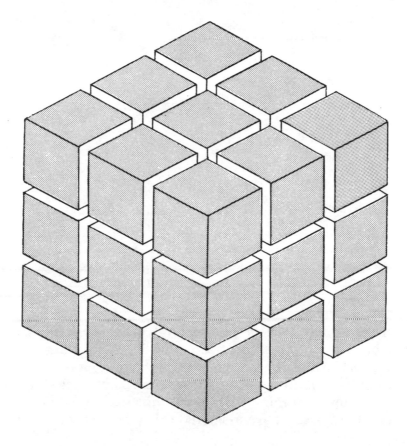

Before this block or cube was subdivided into 27 smaller cubes, it was painted a bright blue on all six of its sides. See if you can answer the following questions concerning the 27 small cubes.

(1) How many cubes have blue paint on three sides?
(2) How many cubes have blue paint on two sides?
(3) How many cubes have blue paint on one side?
(4) How many cubes have no paint on any side?

The World's Best "Tumbler" Puzzle

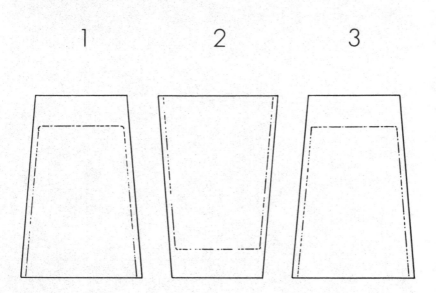

Here's a great "Betcha" puzzle. Line up three tumblers, one mouth down, one mouth up, and the last mouth down. The problem is, *in three moves*, not one, to have all three tumblers' mouths pointing upwards on the table. During each move you must turn two tumblers over, one in each hand. After you have mastered this puzzle, try it on your friends.

The World's Best "Animal" Puzzle

The administrator of a game preserve in Kenya, Africa, decided to take a count of the lions and ostriches he had in one section of the park. For some reason, he did this by counting the number of legs and heads of these animals. He came up with 35 heads and 78 legs. Do you know how many lions there were and how many ostriches?

The World's Best "Horseshoe" Puzzle

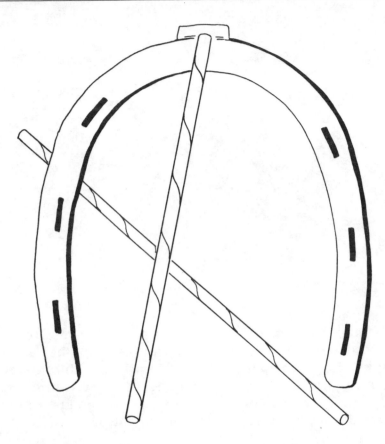

Yes, Virginia, there is a "Horseshoe" puzzle. It's easy to make but hard to solve. Draw a six-inch-high horseshoe on a piece of cardboard and cut it out. Next, take a drinking straw and prop the horseshoe up in a standing position, as shown above. (You may have to trim the straw down a bit.)

Now comes the fun. Take a second straw and, without bending it in any way, use it to pick up both the horseshoe and the straw that is holding it up. You'll get a kick out of this problem!

The World's Best "Mars" Puzzle

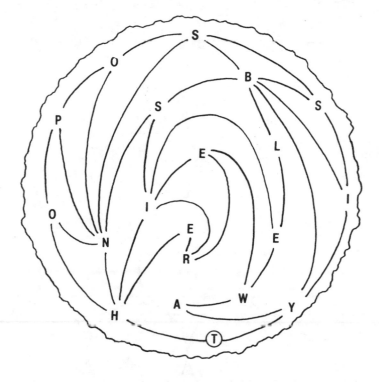

One of the oldest, and best, problems in puzzledom is the "Mars" puzzle by Sam Loyd. Shown here is a map of Mars, *circa* 1900, showing the canals that were thought to exist at that time. At the junctions of these canals are located 20 pumping stations. For the sake of this puzzle the pumping stations have been labelled with letters. If you start at station "T," and make a round-trip tour of all 20 stations, you can spell out a complete English sentence. You must travel along the canals and you cannot visit any station more than once.

When Sam Loyd first published this puzzle, over 50,000 readers wrote in, concerning the solution, that "there is no possible way." See if you can succeed where so many have failed in the past.

The World's Best "Billiard Ball" Puzzle

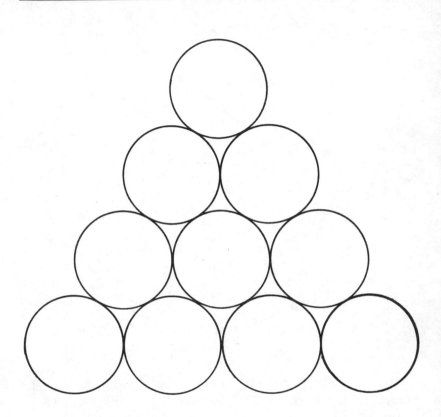

No group of puzzles would be complete without the famous "Billiard Ball" problem. Here we see ten billiard balls racked up on the table with the point of the rack pointing up. Your problem is to move three of the billiard balls to new positions so that the rack of ten balls will now be pointing downwards.

The World's Best "Crossroads" Puzzle

Here we find Napoleon standing literally at the crossroads. During the night, a supply wagon knocked over a signpost at the crossing of two roads. No one in Napoleon's company knows how to replace the signpost so that the arrows will be pointing in the right directions. After contemplating the problem for a few moments, the general issues orders that cause the sign to be replaced correctly. Since Napoleon had never been to this crossroads before, how was he able to do this?

The World's Best "Pegboard" Puzzle

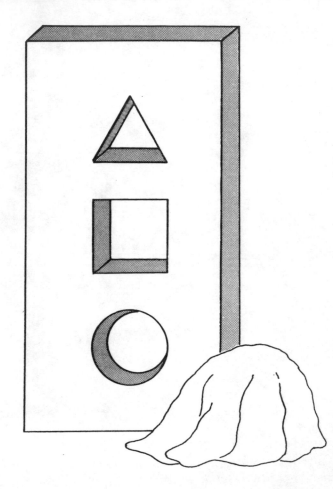

Fitting a square peg into a square hole is easy enough. How about fitting one peg into a square hole, a round hole, and a triangular hole. Impossible, you say! Don't believe it. Hidden under the cloth in the illustration is just such a peg. It will fit snugly into each of the holes shown in the pegboard. Your problem is to figure out the shape of this peg.

The World's Best "Plate" Puzzle

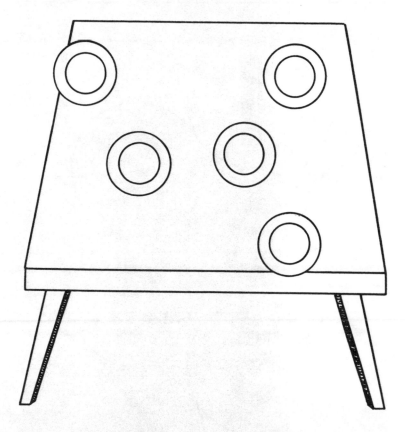

This is more of a game than a puzzle. The object is to cover a table of any size or shape with plates. Each player, in turn, places one plate upon the table. The plates must all be of the same size. When there is no more open space on the table, the last person to have placed a plate down is declared the winner. The plates can overlap the edges of the table.

There is a way of placing the plates that will assure you of winning every time. Also, whether you go first or second can determine whether you'll win or lose. These are the puzzles you are to work out.

The World's Best "Coaster" Puzzle

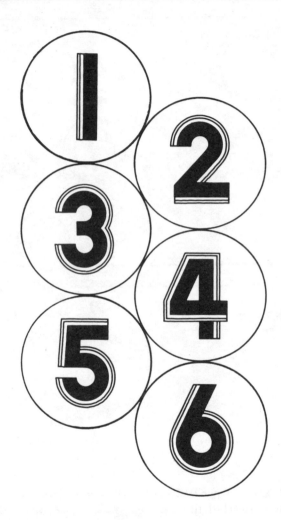

Lay out on a table six round beverage coasters as shown. The coasters should just be touching one another. You must now re-form them into a "perfect" circle by rearranging three of them. When doing this, you are allowed to move only one coaster at a time.

The World's Best "Tinkertoy" Puzzle

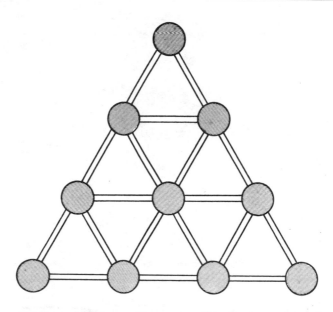

Here is a puzzle construction made using Tinkertoy rods and connectors. The construction is made up of nine equal-sized triangles. Your problem is to remove five of these rods in such a way that you will be left with five equal triangles.

The World's Best "Cork" Puzzle

Now here's a "corking" good puzzle for you to solve. Fill a glass two-thirds full of water and drop a small cork into it. Challenge anyone present to make the cork float exactly in the middle of the glass for five minutes. No matter how hard they try, the cork will always slowly drift to one side.

There is, however, a surefire method that will cause the cork to float dead on center. *Note*: Nothing is used in the solution but the glass, the water, and the cork.

The World's Best "Hat" Puzzle

This is both a trick and a puzzle. Place three peanuts on a table, spacing them one foot apart. Next, place a hat over each peanut. This should be done in complete silence with slow, precise moves. Return to the first hat. Lift it up, place the peanut in your mouth and chew it up. Replace the hat. Repeat your actions with the second hat, and then with the third hat. Look at your audience and declare that you will now cause the three peanuts to come together under any one of the three hats. As soon as a hat is chosen, you immediately do this.

How do you accomplish this impossible feat?

The World's Best "Age" Puzzle

"Mind your manners, you old coot! I'm over 21, and that's all the information about my age that you're going to get!"

If "Swifty" Armbruster really wants to know Miss Prim's age, he should ask her what her shoe size is. That's right, you can determine anyone's age by the size of the gunboats that they wear. Do you know how to do it?

The World's Best "Record" Puzzle

33 RPM

78 RPM

45 RPM

This is really a "groovy" puzzle. Shown here are three phonograph records: a 12-inch, 33 RPM record; a 10-inch, 78 RPM record; and a 7-inch, 45 RPM record. Can you guess how many grooves there are in each record? Your answers must be within 100 grooves of each record's total to be considered correct.

The World's Best "Marble" Puzzle

Place a glass jar on the upturned palm of someone's hand. Next, drop a marble into the jar. Now, challenge your assistant to grip the bottom of the jar, turn the jar mouth downwards, walk across the room and place the jar, still mouth downwards, on the top of a table. The one catch in all of this is that the marble must not fall out of the jar. You cannot place anything over the mouth of the jar, or push anything into the jar to hold the marble in place. The only items allowed in this puzzle are the assistant's hand, the glass jar, and the marble.

The World's Best "Pyramid" Puzzle

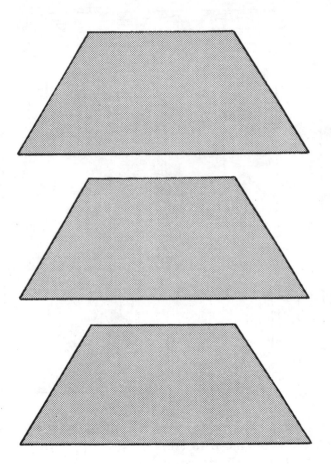

We have what looks like three pieces of a jigsaw puzzle. Your problem is to arrange the pieces into one figure that will resemble a pyramid (the shape of a triangle).

If you trace the figures onto a piece of cardboard and cut them out, you will have an interesting puzzle to stump your friends with.

The World's Best "Circle" Puzzle

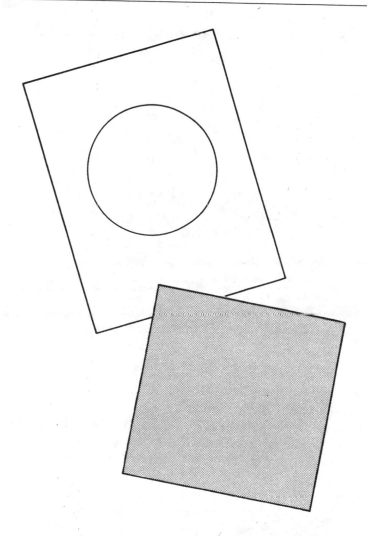

If you wanted to find the center of a circle, and all you had to work with was a pencil and a square piece of cardboard, larger than the circle, how would you go about solving the problem? It's really easier than it looks. You have five minutes to find the solution.

The World's Best "Dream" Puzzle

Mr. Adams looked up from a book he was reading on famous dreams and said to his wife: "Dear, listen to this story! It's really quite amazing!"

"Boston, Mass., April 1, 1903. Mr. K— had the following dream. Having gone to bed after reading a book about King Arthur's Court, Mr. K— dreamt that he was fighting in a joust against the dreaded Black Knight. He had been thrown from his horse, and as he lay dazed upon the ground, the Black Knight came thundering towards him with his lance aimed straight at Mr. K—'s middle. At this point, his wife woke up, and seeing her husband was having a nightmare, she poked him in the stomach in an attempt to wake him up. At this, her husband screamed in his sleep, clutched his stomach, and fell back onto the bed dead of a heart attack."

"All I can say, Martha, is never wake me up in the middle of a nightmare," finished Mr. Adams.

"That's quite a tale, all right, Amos," replied Martha, "but I don't believe a word of it. Any fool can see that that's a made-up story."

How did Martha know that the story was a phony?

The World's Best "Postal" Puzzle

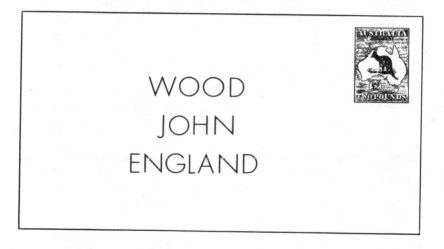

This letter is said to have been sent to a gentleman in Great Britain. Believe it or not, the letter was promptly delivered to the addressee. Can you decipher the complete address?

The World's Best "Rune Stone" Puzzle

A recently discovered "Rune Stone," near Husavik, Iceland, had archaeologists running around in circles until a young schoolboy pointed out to them that the stone was obviously a fake since it depicted a well-known puzzle. Chiselled into the stone were nine cryptic characters. The sixth character, the third one in the middle row, was purposely left unfinished. The puzzle, then, is to figure out what this character should be. This can be done by determining what each of the other characters stands for. *Hint:* All of the characters have something in common.

The World's Best "Truck" Puzzle

The story goes that many years ago a truck driver was flagged down by a policeman and told that his truck had to be checked for overloading. As soon as the driver had driven his truck onto the weighing machine, he jumped out of the cab and started pounding the side of the truck with a piece of wood. A bystander asked the driver why he was doing that.

"Well," he replied, "I'm carrying 5,000 pounds of live canaries in the truck. I know that my truck is overloaded, but if I can keep the birds flying around inside the truck their weight won't show up on the scales."

Is what the driver said true? If the birds are kept flying inside the enclosed box of the truck, will the truck really weigh less than if the birds were sitting on their perches?

The World's Best "Betting" Puzzle

"J. Wellington Moneybags is my name, and gambling is my game. I'll bet on anything, anytime, anywhere. Why, I'll even bet you that I can cut a hole in an ordinary playing card and step right through it. I'm not kidding! I'll pass my entire body, all 230 pounds of me, through a hole in a playing card without ripping the card apart. That's my wager. Who would like to bet me a hundred dollars that I can't do it?"

Don't take him up on it, readers! If J. Wellington says he can do something, believe him. They don't call him the "Ace of Gamblers" for nothing. However, it would be interesting to know how he would do it. Any ideas?

The World's Best "Bottle" Puzzle

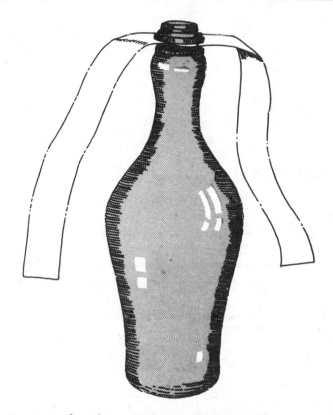

Place an empty bottle upright on the table. Next, cut a one-inch-wide strip of paper, one foot long, from a newspaper. Place the strip of paper over the mouth of the bottle as shown. Finally, place four coins on top of the paper. Start with a quarter, then add a nickel and two pennies. Now, challenge anyone to remove the strip of paper leaving the coins still balanced on top of the bottle. They cannot touch either the coins or the bottle while doing this. The only item that may be touched, in any way, by anything, is the strip of paper. Your friends will soon discover that this problem is nearly impossible to solve. Try it a few times yourself before looking up the answer.

The World's Best "Find-The-Wife" Puzzle

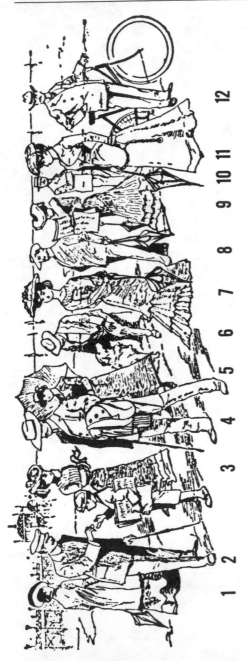

Six men and six women are strolling on a beach during the summer of 1903. Nos. 1, 3, 5, 7, 9, and 11 are women, and Nos. 2, 4, 6, 8, 10, and 12 are men. These 12 individuals represent 6 married couples, who, in walking aimlessly about, have gotten mixed up. You have to find the wife of the man wearing the straw hat—No. 10. By examining the 6 ladies carefully and diligently searching for clues, you can eliminate all but the lady in question.

The following clues have a bearing on how the puzzle is solved: (1) one of the ladies is dressed for cycling, (2) buttons on a coat, (3) newspapers, (4) the dog, (5) parasols.

The World's Best "X-Ray" Puzzle

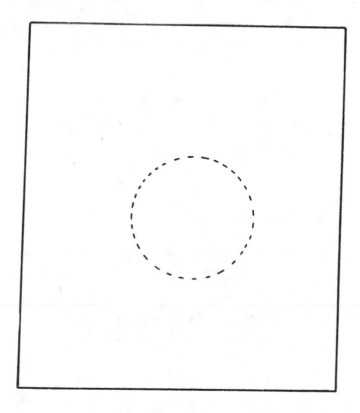

Turn your back and instruct anyone present to place a silver dollar, face up, on top of the table. Next, tell them to place a square piece of blank paper over the coin. Now, turn around and declare that you will use your superpowers to look right through the sheet of opaque paper and read the date on the coin. State that at no time will the paper be lifted from the coin, and that the coin will be fully covered at all times. Just to make things more interesting, propose the following wager. If you succeed in reading the date, you get to keep the coin. If you fail, he gets to keep it. Sounds fair to me!

The World's Best "Frog" Puzzle

There is a story told of a frog that fell off his bicycle and ended up at the bottom of a ten-foot well. The well was too deep to hop out of, so the frog started to climb up the slippery sides. Every day he was able to climb up three feet, but during the night, while he rested, he slid back down two feet. At this rate, how many days did it take for the famous "Climbing Frog of Clavicle County" to get out of that well?

The World's Best "Hotel" Puzzle

Here's a neat turn-of-the-century puzzle. Three gentlemen checked into a hotel and asked for three separate rooms. They were charged a total of $30 for the night. In the morning, the desk clerk discovered that he should have only charged them $25 for the three rooms. He gave the bellboy five dollars and told him to return the money to the gentlemen. The bellboy, being of a dishonest nature, pocketed two dollars and gave the gentlemen back three dollars. Everyone was now happy except a puzzle solver who heard about the transactions. Since the lodgers only paid $27 for the night, and the bellboy kept two dollars for himself, whatever happened to the last dollar of the original $30 paid to the clerk the night before? Can you unravel this mystery?

The World's Best "Pilsner Glass" Puzzle

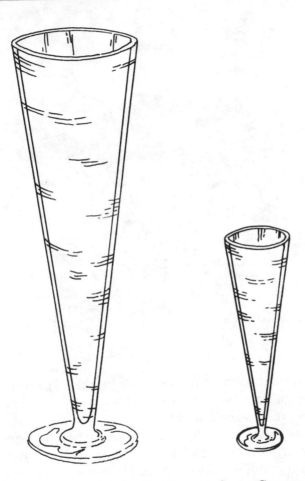

Shown here are two Pilsner glasses from Germany. The inside dimensions of the larger glass are exactly twice as great as the inside dimensions of the smaller glass. What we want to do is fill the larger glass with water using the smaller glass as a measure. We fill the smaller glass with water and then pour the water into the larger glass. The question is: How many times will we have to do this to completely fill the larger glass?

The World's Best "Sea Shell" Puzzle

The next time you're at the seashore, try playing this game on the beach. Lay out five rows of five sea shells each in the sand. Each player, in turn, may remove one or more shells from any row or column. However, there cannot be a gap between any of the sea shells. The sea shells must be next to one another within the row or column you are removing them from. Suppose the first player removes shells 3 and 4 from the top row of shells. His opponent could not then remove shells 1, 2, and 5 from this row because there would be a gap between shells 2 and 5. The player could, however, remove shells 1 and 2, or shell 5 from this row. The person who is forced to remove the last shell from the board is the *loser* of the game.

Note: Since this is a game instead of a puzzle, there is no solution.

The World's Best "Policeman" Puzzle

At the turn of the century Olaf Anderson became a policeman in a small city. He was assigned a beat in the city that covered six square blocks. Being a conscientious policeman, Officer Anderson wished to find the shortest possible route he could take that would enable him to circle each block during one complete trip around his beat. In the answer section, the route that he worked out is given. We think that it's the best possible solution. However, there just may be a shorter route, so give it a try before checking out the answer.

The World's Best "Lemonade" Puzzle

"But, but, your honor . . . !"

Three English brothers received a rather strange inheritance when a beloved uncle passed away. He willed them 21 barrels of lemonade. On examining the legacy, they found that seven of the barrels were full, seven were half-full, and the remaining seven were empty. The will stipulated that each of the brothers was to get an equal share of full, half-full, and empty lemonade barrels. In court, a problem arose over the simplest method to be used to accomplish the terms of the will. The judge proposed that the sons throw a party and drink up all of the lemonade and then divide up the empty barrels. However, their barrister, Trevor Torts, held out for a better solution than that. Can you come up with a solution where, using only the barrels for measuring the liquid, you can divide both the lemonade and the barrels equally among the three brothers?

The World's Best "Real Estate" Puzzle

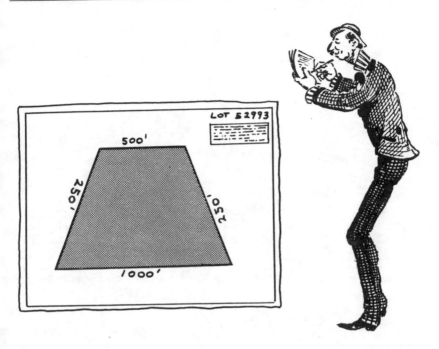

Slippery Sidney, a dealer in underwater acreage, was try-ing to close a fast deal on a piece of sight-unseen land.

"You'll love this lot," he said. "It has a beautiful view of the ocean. And, it will only cost you $25,000 for all these acres of shorefront property."

"That's what I want to know," replied Gullible George. "Just how many acres of land am I getting for my money? Let me see that map again. First I have to figure out how many square feet of land is in the lot, and then I'll have to divide this amount by the number of square feet in an acre. By the way, Sidney, how many square feet are there in an acre?"

"Well, ahem, there are 43,560 square feet in an acre, but why bother figuring it out? Take my word for it. You're going to make out like a bandit on this deal."

Do you think George is getting a "square deal" or a "raw deal" from Sidney? Check the map of the lot and see just how many acres he would get for his money.

The World's Best "Crystal" Puzzle

"All right, gentlemen, please pay attention. The first one who can tell me how to fill a crystal goblet with water from that crystal water pitcher, and yet leave the pitcher with exactly the same amount of water in it as before, shall have the first dance with me at the Yacht Club's Cotillion Ball!"

"Er, ah, ahem . . . how about giving us a clue, Daph?"

"I say, Daphne, could you run through that again, please?"

Can you perform this seemingly impossible feat and win the young lady's attention?

The World's Best "Jealous Husband" Puzzle

Three jealous husbands travelling with their wives found it necessary to cross a stream in a boat which held only two persons. Each of the husbands had a great objection to his wife crossing with either of the other male members of the party unless he himself was also present. They also objected to leaving their wives alone with the other husbands on either side of the stream.

How was the passage arranged? Remember, though the boat held two people, one of them had to bring the boat back for the rest of the people to use.

The World's Best "Bicycle" Puzzle

When bicycling was in its infancy, two young cyclists, Betty and Nadine Parkhurst, set out one day to visit their aunt in the country some 20 miles away. After they had covered four miles, Betty's bike broke down and she had to chain it to a tree. Being in a hurry, they decided to push on as quickly as they could. They had the choice of both walking, or of one walking and one riding the remaining bike. They both could walk at the rate of four miles an hour and ride at eight miles an hour. They decided on a plan of action that would keep their walking to a minimum and yet would get them to their aunt's house in the shortest amount of time. What combination of walking and riding did they use?

The World's Best "Testing" Puzzle

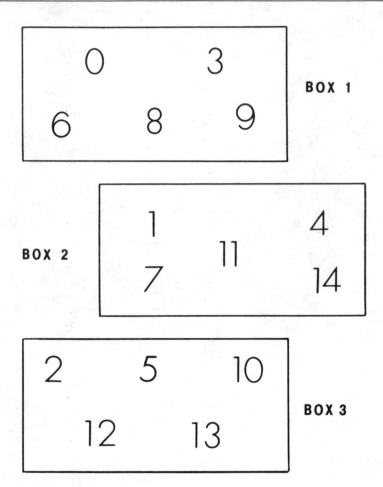

Here's an interesting testing problem for you. Arranged in the three boxes are the numbers 0 through 14. The "tester" has placed the numbers in each box according to some scheme he has made up. The problem is to reason this scheme out so that you can place the next three numbers, 15, 16, and 17, into the correct boxes. Your time limit on this test is five minutes.

The World's Best "Deductive" Puzzle

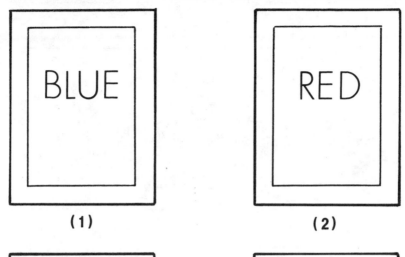

(1) (2)

(3)

(4)

From two old packs of Australian playing cards, one with blue backs and the other with red backs, we have selected four cards and placed two of them faceup and the other two facedown on the table. Now here's the problem: "Does every blue-backed card on the table have a king on its other side?"

To solve this puzzle, you are allowed to turn two of the cards over. Which two cards would you turn over?

The World's Best "Tennis" Puzzle

Many years ago, at the Idle Hours Country Club, they had a super turnout for the Teddy Roosevelt Mixed Doubles Tennis Tournament. One hundred and twenty-eight couples registered for the big event. Thaddeus Rackencut, the groundskeeper, was up half the night drawing up the schedule board. Do you know how many doubles matches were played before a winner was determined?

The World's Best "Liquid" Puzzle

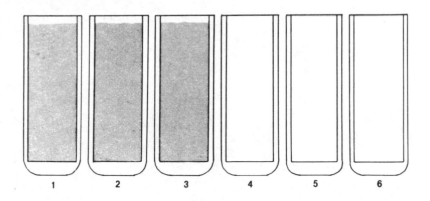

Here's a neat "challenge" puzzle. Line up six glasses in a row on your table. The first three glasses are filled with water while the next three are empty. The problem is to change the order of the glasses so that the first glass is filled with water, the second is empty, the third is filled, the fourth is empty, the fifth is filled and the sixth is empty. In doing this, you are only allowed to move one of the glasses. It looks impossible, but in this case looks are deceiving.

The World's Best "Nail" Puzzle

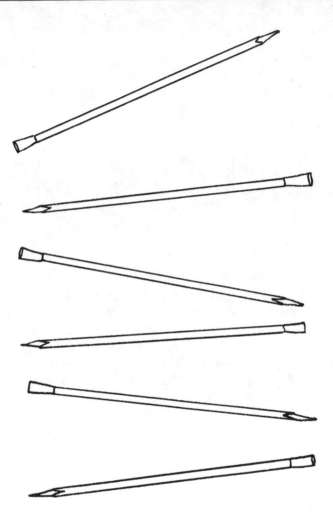

Here's an old carpenter's puzzle. You have to arrange six finishing nails so that each nail touches every other nail. It sounds easy, but watch out; you may be the one that's "finished" before you give up on this one.

The World's Best "Knickknack" Puzzle

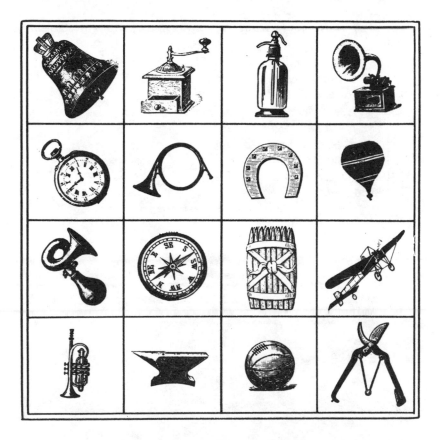

Shown above are items on shelves in the window of Ye Olde Knickknack Shoppe. You are to remove any six of the items so that the remaining ten will be distributed evenly in the four columns and rows that make up the window display. There must be an even number of objects in each horizontal and vertical row, as well as in the two corner diagonal rows. Try working this puzzle using coins or checkers. The answer section contains one of many solutions that have been worked out for this particular problem in the past.

The World's Best "Travelling" Puzzle

"All right now, Alfred, pay attention! I'll repeat the puzzle one more time.
    'As I was going to St. Ives,
    I met a man with seven wives,
    Each wife had seven sacks,
    Each sack had seven cats,
    Each cat had seven kits;
    Kits, cats, sacks, and wives,
    How many were there going to St. Ives?'
It's really not very hard if you give it a little thought."

This poem is a favorite among puzzle solvers. Can you figure it out before Alfred and his friend reach their destinations?

The World's Best "Number" Puzzle

Shown here are two columns of four cards each. Can you rearrange two of these cards so that the sum of the four numbers in each row will be the same? (Right now the sums are 19 and 20.)

The World's Best "Antique" Puzzle

The other day Calvin Collectible, an antique dealer, bought a cast-iron fountain, depicting a crocodile swallowing a fish. For this marvellous work of art (?), he paid 90 percent of its "book" value. The next day, another collector saw it and offered to buy it from him for 25 percent above its book value. Calvin, no slouch at turning a quick buck, accepted the offer and made a nice profit of $105 over his purchase price. With these facts to work with, can you determine what the book value of this bubbling curiosity is?

The World's Best "Mr. T" Puzzle

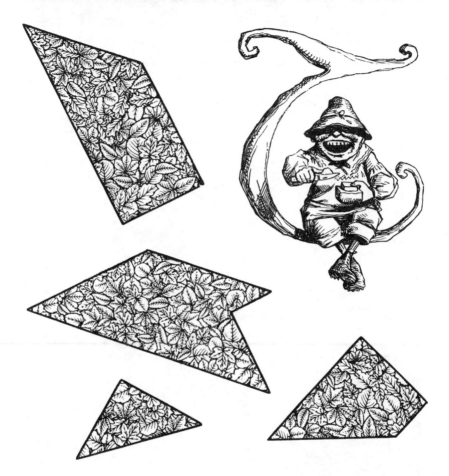

Is this gnome laughing at you because he doesn't think you'll be able to solve the "Mr. T" puzzle? Could be! Trace the four pieces of the puzzle onto a piece of construction paper and cut them out. Now, all you have to do is re-arrange them to form a perfect capital T. Sounds easy, but the T leaves above tell me that you're in for a big surprise!

The World's Best "Fly" Puzzle

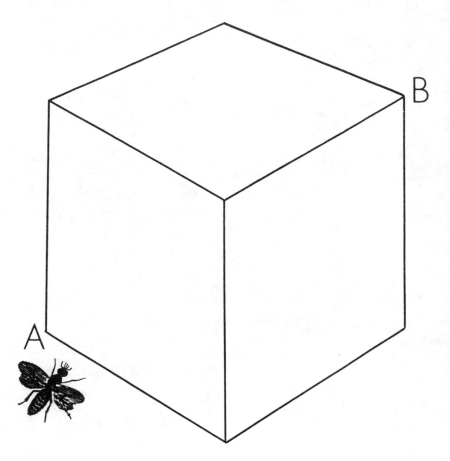

That educated fly that has appeared in so many puzzles is back for another try at stumping our readers. This time he has discovered a marble pedestal that he would like to negotiate. He wants to travel from point A, the left lower corner of the cube shown here, to point B, the upper right corner on the opposite side of the cube. The cube measures exactly two feet along each of its edges. Can you figure out the shortest possible route for our friendly fly to take?

The World's Best "Marching" Puzzle

The year is 1895 and subaltern Henry Faversham, of the British army, is being interviewed by Maude Muckraker for the *Independent London Times*. It looks as if Maude is having her doubts about the yarn young Henry is spinning. He claims that on a recent hike his outfit, starting at some undisclosed part of the world, marched due south for 100 miles, then due east for 200 miles, turned once again and marched due north for 100 miles and ended up back where it had started from.

"Impossible," snorts Maude, terminating the interview. "What you claim, young man, is patently impossible!"

Is Maude wrong, or is there a spot on earth where Henry could have carried out the march? Can you tell us where this exotic place is located?

The World's Best "Racing" Puzzle

Two sporting gentlemen decided to stage a race where the buggy that crossed the finish line first would *lose* and the one that came in second would win. Off they went, down a one-mile course, whipping their horses to a lather. As they neared the finish line, they both slowed down until they came to a halt with only 100 yards to go. Realizing that they had made a dumb bet, the two drivers got down and went over to discuss the matter with a farmer who was watching them from his field. When the farmer heard their story, he gave them a piece of advice that sent them leaping into the buggies and speeding down the course, as each one strained to be the first to cross the finish line.

The advice that the farmer gave them in no way changed the terms of the original wager. Can you guess what it was?

The World's Best "Tire" Puzzle

Herbie Glencove has just returned from a transcontinental motor tour in his new Stanley Steamer. All told, he clocked a total of 6,275 miles during the trip. He carried one spare tire, which he rotated from wheel to wheel. Herbie figures that each one of the five tires on his car was used equally during the trip. Can you figure out how many miles of wear each tire accumulated?

The World's Best "Brain Teaser" Puzzle

Here are three facedown playing cards numbered 1, 2, and 3. Your job is to figure out the value and suit of each playing card. To help you in this exercise in pure deduction, the following four clues are given:

(1) There is at least one 3 immediately to the right of a 2.
(2) There is at least one club immediately to the right of a club.
(3) There is at least one 3 immediately to the left of a 3.
(4) There is at least one club immediately to the left of a diamond.

The World's Best "Candle" Puzzle

The town of Haywood was founded back in 1867 by Hamilton Haywood. Uncle Hay, as he was known to all, became a very rich man. Some say that this was because he was also a very frugal individual. As an example, Uncle Hay found out that instead of throwing away the stubs of used candles you could melt them down and turn them into new candles. It turned out that one new candle could be made out of four candle stubs. Since Uncle Hay bought all of his candles in Handy-Paks of 16, how many new candles was he able to make from each package?

The World's Best "Cookie" Puzzle

Little Ariadne is very upset. Earlier in the day she received a package of fresh, homemade cookies from her mother. As she was opening her gift, four of her friends arrived and reminded Ariadne that they had shared their cookies with her and that it was now her turn to pay them back. Reluctantly, she counted out and gave half of her cookies and half a cookie to her friend Lorella. To Melva, she gave half of what was left and half a cookie. Then she counted out half of the remaining cookies and half a cookie, and gave them to Laureen. To the last girl, Margot, she handed half of what was left in the box and half a cookie. This left poor Ariadne with an empty cookie box and mayhem in her heart.

Can you figure out how many cookies were originally in the box? By the way, at no time did Ariadne cut up or break in two any of the cookies in the box.

The World's Best "Archaeology" Puzzle

Around the turn of the century two archaeologists made an interesting discovery.

"Well, there it is, Petrie," said one archaeologist to the other, "the greatest find in a hundred years. A giant Greek amphora almost 2,000 years old, and in perfect condition. See, it's even engraved with the year it was made, 17 B.C. Another interesting thing about it is the inscription on the front. It says: 'This vessel is the property of Pylos, Mighty Wizard of Corinth. It contains the strongest chemical on earth. The chemical was created by Pylos and is so strong that it will dissolve anything that it comes in contact with. The name of this chemical is . . .' Drat, the rest of the inscription is indecipherable. Anyway, what do you think of my find?"

"Frankly, Hawkings, I think you've gone crackers!" thundered Petrie. "Any first-year student on his first dig would see that your 'find' was a fake. After looking at it, and reading that inscription, I can point out three errors in it right away."

Can you spot the errors in this "Find of the Century"?

The World's Best "Horn" Puzzle

One year Groucho Marx bought a new horn for his brother Harpo's birthday. After having it wrapped, he took it to the post office to mail.

"I'm sorry, Mr. Marx," said the postal clerk, "but this package is too long. Regulations state that no package can be more than four feet long. This one is five feet in length."

Groucho took the horn and returned to the shop. They removed the rubber bulb, but the horn was still four feet eight inches long. Then Groucho had an idea. He had them rewrap the horn in a different way. When he returned to the post office they accepted his package because it was now regulation size. How did he do it? Remember, the horn was not cut, or bent out of shape, in any way.

The World's Best "Wallet" Puzzle

Mr. Willard Gotrocks rushed into the police station the other day shouting that his wallet had been stolen.

"Hold on now, Mr. Gotrocks," said Sergeant Anderson. "Someone just turned in a wallet. Maybe it's yours. Can you identify its contents?"

"Well," replied Willard, "there's a picture of W.C. Fields in it, and there's my 'Everything' credit card. Oh, yes, I had exactly $63 in cash in six bills, and none of them was a $1 bill."

"That clinches it, Mr. Gotrocks. Here's your wallet."

Can you calculate what six bills he had in his wallet that added up to exactly $63?

ANSWERS

Answers

"Farm" puzzle (page 8). Hiram found that if he laid out each parcel of land in the shape of an "L" (A), he could neatly subdivide his farm into four equal plots (B).

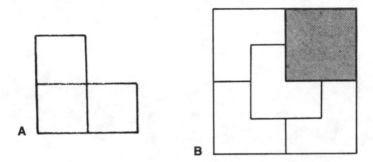

A

B

"Bully" puzzle (page 8). Take your opponent over to a doorway and lay the handkerchief across the opening so that half of it is in each room. Have your opponent enter the other room and stand on the edge of the handkerchief. Now close the door, which should open into the room, and lock it. Finally, move up and stand on the edge of the handkerchief that is in your room. You can now safely dare your friend in a loud voice to take a swing at you, as you are now ready for the best he can dish out.

"Monument" puzzle (page 9). The illustration shows the side view of the monument.

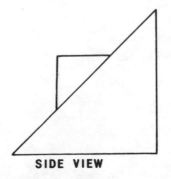

SIDE VIEW

"Window" puzzle (page 10). See the illustration. The shaded area is the part of the window that is painted blue.

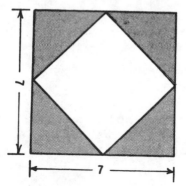

"Soda Straw" puzzle (page 10). Tightly fold the straw about three inches from one end so that it forms a "V." Insert this end of the straw into the bottle and maneuver it around until it gets wedged in the bottle. When this happens, you will be able to lift the bottle off the table. See the illustration.

"Fish Tank" puzzle (page 11). Tip one end of the tank up into the air, letting the water spill out over the other side. Continue this until the water level runs from one bottom corner to the top of the opposite side. At this point, the tank will be exactly half full of water. It's a messy solution, but it works.

"Coin" puzzle (page 12). The moves are: (1) 5 to 8, remove 7; (2) 2 to 5, remove 4; (3) 9 to 2, remove 6; (4) 10 to 6, remove 8; (5) 1 to 4, remove 2; (6) 3 to 7, remove 4; (7) 5 to 8, remove 7; (8) 6 to 10, remove 8.

"Matchstick" puzzle (page 13). The illustration shows the two squares that remain when you remove eight matchsticks.

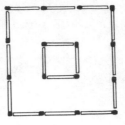

"Line" puzzle (page 14).
The illustration shows how
to draw the kite without
crossing the lines at any
point or going over any part
of the line more than once.

"Book" puzzle (page 15). To break the string below the
book, give the string a sharp downward jerk. You will be
pulling against the inertia of the two-pound book, and the
string should break before any of this force is transmitted
to the string above the book. To break the string above the
book, pull slowly on the string. The force exerted, plus the
weight of the book, will cause the string above the book to
snap first.

**"Ice-Cream-Stick" puzzle (page
16).** Slide the stick on the "bottom"
of the glass partway to the left.
Then move the stick that is on the
"right" side of the glass to the left of
the glass stem. The glass is now
upside down, and the cherry is on
the outside. See the illustration.

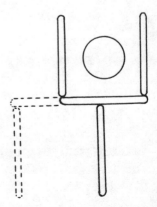

"Pizza" puzzle (page 17). Slice the pie in half. Slice it in half again in the other direction. You now have four quarters (A). Stack the four pieces on top of each other. Cut this stack in half with your third cut. You now have eight pieces (B).

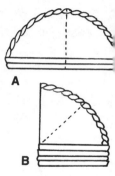

"Counting" puzzle (page 18). There are 44 triangles of several different sizes. Many of them overlap in part other triangles in the illustration. Below are three different types of triangles that appear in the geometric figure.

"Toothpick" puzzle (page 19). Move the three toothpicks denoted by broken lines in the fish at the left (A) and replace them in the positions indicated by the broken lines in the fish on the right (B).

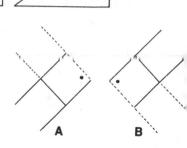

"Rope" puzzle (page 20). Pass the loop of your rope through the loop which encircles one of your friend's wrists, slide it over the hand, and pass it back again through the loop. The ropes will now be separated.

"Stamp" puzzle (page 21). Place two stamps, one on top of the other, in the middle of the cross. There are now "four" stamps in each line of the cross. See the illustration.

"Ice Cube" puzzle (page 22). Lay the middle of the string across the top of the ice cube. Now, pour a quantity of salt on top of the string and ice (practice will show you just how much). The salt will cause the ice under the string to melt. In turn, as the salt water flows off the top of the cube, the water will freeze around the string, making it stick to the ice. After a few minutes, you will be able to lift the string and the ice cube out of the glass.

"Spelling" puzzle (page 23). The countries are as follow: (1) POLAND, (2) SCOTLAND, (3) BULGARIA, (4) NEPAL, (5) ENGLAND, (6) RUMANIA, and (7) PAKISTAN.

"Train" puzzle (page 24). It's simple. One train entered the tunnel at two o'clock in the morning, while the other train entered the tunnel at two o'clock in the afternoon.

"Paper" puzzle (page 24). Fold the paper across the middle of the hole. Place the quarter on top of the hole, fold the two sides of the paper together, and pick it up as shown in the illustration. Now, bend the corners of the paper towards each other. The hole will enlarge, without tearing, around the quarter and it will fall through.

"Hardware Shop" puzzle (page 25). The builder of the condos had forgotten to place their house numbers on each unit. Down at the hardware shop, they sell these numbers for $1.00 each. Since there are only nine units in the Friar Briar Estates, no condo will need more than one number. Therefore, four buyers will buy four numbers for a total sale of $4.00.

"Dime" puzzle (page 26). Place your forefinger on the table opposite the dime, and scratch the cloth lightly. The dime will move slowly in the opposite direction. Soon it will come out from under the glass.

"Arrowhead" puzzle (page 27). If you place the four arrowheads on the table as shown in the illustration, you will "see" a fifth arrowhead outlined in the middle. That answer should send a "quiver" up your spine.

"Yardstick" puzzle (page 28). When you move your fingers away from the ends to the middle of the yardstick, it is friction that causes them to meet exactly at the middle. First, one finger will stick and the other will slide towards the middle. As the finger gets closer to the middle, it supports more of the yardstick's weight. Soon friction causes this finger to stick while the other one begins to slide. This situation continues back and forth until both fingers reach the middle together.

When starting from the middle and moving out towards the ends, one finger will always have slightly less friction than the other. As this finger moves away from the middle, more of the weight of the ruler is transferred to the finger still at the middle; this makes it even easier for the moving finger to go all the way to the end.

"Paper Clip" puzzle (page 28). All you have to do is grasp the bill by both ends and smartly snap it apart. The paper clips will fly off, firmly linked together. Amazing, but true!

"Checkerboard" puzzle (page 29). The illustration on the following page shows one of the many solutions to the puzzle.

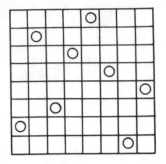

"Sugar" puzzle (page 30). This is a puzzle with a "catch" to it. Place one lump of sugar in cup one, two lumps in cup two, and three lumps in cup three. Finally, pick up cup three and place it in cup two. Now each cup has an "odd" number of sugar cubes in it.

"Dollar Bill" puzzle (page 31). Though it looks easy to catch the dollar bill, it's impossible to do it more than once in ten tries. Your reflexes are just not fast enough.

"Clock" puzzle (page 32). Adding up the numbers in the upper half of the clockface, 10, 11, 12, 1, 2, and 3, we get a total count of 39. Adding up the numbers in the lower half, 9, 8, 7, 6, 5, and 4, we also get a total count of 39.

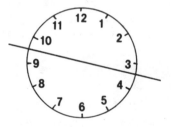

"Money" puzzle (page 32). The problem states that the bottle contains an equal number of quarters, half-dollars and silver dollars. Let's say that n represents this number. Therefore: $(.25 \times n)$ and $(.50 \times n)$ and $(\$1.00 \times n) = \$700$. We can refine this equation and say:

$\$1.75 \times n = \$700; n = \dfrac{\$700}{\$1.75;} n = 400.$

So there are exactly 400 quarters, 400 half-dollars and 400 silver dollars in the bottle.

"Cannonball" puzzle (page 33). Soldier Duncan will need exactly 30 more cannonballs in four levels to complete his pyramid. The first level contains 16 cannonballs, the second 9, the third 4, and the top level 1.

"Card" puzzle (page 34). The moves are as follow: (1) card 4 on card 1; (2) card 6 on card 9; (3) card 8 on card 3; (4) card 2 on card 7; and (5) card 5 on card 10.

"Illusion" puzzle (page 35). Surprising as it may seem, you will find, by carefully measuring the heights of the animals, that the nearest ones are really either taller than those that follow, or fully equal to them in size. The reason that the latter look so much larger than they really are is that they do not grow smaller in proportion to their surroundings, as does everything else.

"Bookworm" puzzle (page 36). The total distance travelled is 2½ inches. Since the bookworm starts at page one of volume 1, which is on the right side of the book, and heads towards volume 3, the first thing he will start chewing on will be the cover of volume 1. Once through this cover, he will chew through the back cover of volume 2, then on through 2 inches of pages, through the cover of volume 2, and, finally, through the back cover of volume 3, where he will come to the last page of the book, the finish line of our puzzle. This totals four covers and the contents of one volume, or 2½ inches of delicious grazing.

"Chess" puzzle (page 37).

	White		Black
1.	18-15	1.	3- 6
2.	17- 8	2.	4-13
3.	19-14	3.	2- 7
4.	15- 5	4.	6-16
5.	8- 3	5.	13-18
6.	14- 9	6.	7-12
7.	5-10	7.	16-11
8.	9-19	8.	12- 2
9.	10- 4	9.	11-17
10.	20-10	10.	1-11
11.	3- 9	11.	18-12
12.	10-13	12.	11- 8
13.	19-16	13.	2- 5
14.	16- 1	14.	5-20
15.	9- 6	15.	12-15
16.	13- 7	16.	8-14
17.	6- 3	17.	15-18
18.	7- 2	18.	14-19

"Code" puzzle (page 38). First spy: "Did you get my photos of the enemy's new secret weapon?" Second spy: "Yes, you dolt! It turned out to be a plan for a new electric eggbeater."

To break the code, write the 26 letters of the alphabet, "A" through "Z," across the paper. Under them write the letters of the alphabet in reverse order, "Z" through "A." Find each letter, in the coded sentences, in the bottom reversed line of letters and substitute the letter above it in the first line. That's all there is to it.

A B C D E F G H I J K L M N O P Q R S T U V W X Y Z
Z Y X W V U T S R Q P O N M L K J I H G F E D C B A

"Magic Square" puzzle (page 39).

8	3	4
1	5	9
6	7	2

"Geometry" puzzle (page 40). Line OD is the radius of the circle and is six inches long. Figure ABCO is a rectangle whose opposite corners touch the center of the circle and the edge of the circle. Therefore, a radius line OB would be six inches long. Since both diagonals of a rectangle will have the same length, line AC will be equal to line OB, or six inches in length.

"Starship" puzzle (page 41). Take the following route: Starting at command center 2, go E, N, H, 3, J, N, M, 4, L, 3, G, 2, C, 1, B, N, K, 3, I, N, F, 2, D, N, A, 1.

"Archery" puzzle (page 42). To score exactly 100, using six arrows, put them in the following target rings: 16, 16, 17, 17, 17, 17.

"Dice" puzzle (page 43). After the first die is in the cup, *do not* toss the second die into the air. This is what causes all the problems. Instead, release the die and quickly drop your hand, with the cup, down and under the die so that it falls neatly into the cup. It's really pretty easy.

"Button" puzzle (page 44). Here are the moves (W = white and R = red): (1) W2 to 3; (2) R4 to 2; (3) R5 to 4; (4) W3 to 5; (5) W1 to 3; (6) R2 to 1; (7) R4 to 2; and (8) W3 to 4.

"Progression" puzzle (page 45). For the first series of letters, each letter is the beginning of the numbers one, two, three, four, and five. The next three letters would be "S," "S," and "E."

For the second series of letters, each letter is the beginning of the days Sunday, Monday, Tuesday, Wednesday, and Thursday. The next two letters would be "F" and "S."

For the third series of letters, each letter is the beginning of the months of the year in reverse order: December, November, October, September, August. The next three letters are "J," "J," and "M."

"Chain" puzzle (page 46). Since there are six sections of chain, the solution that comes to mind first is to open the end link on one chain and reclose it around the end link of another chain. Doing this five times would join all six sections together at a total cost of $6.25.

However, there is an even cheaper way to solve this puzzle. Take the chain with four links and have each link opened. This will cost 75¢ times 4, or $3.00. Use these four links to join the remaining five sections of chain together. Welding these four links shut will cost an additional $2.00. Our total cost for creating one chain, with 29 links, will be just $5.00.

"Footprint" puzzle (page 47). Who said that the answer is as clear as mud? Anyone can see that those tracks were made by a one-legged man with a peg leg pushing a wheelbarrow.

"Word" puzzle (page 48). The words are as follow: (1) Sidewalk, (2) Sitting Bull, (3) Hopscotch, (4) Fast Break, (5) Clipboard, and (6) Drop Kick.

"Block" puzzle (page 49). The answers are as follow:
(1) 3 sides painted blue =   8 cubes
(2) 2 sides painted blue = 12 cubes
(3) 1 side painted blue   =   6 cubes
(4) no paint on any side =   1 cube
    Total   = 27 cubes

"Tumbler puzzle (page 50). First move: Turn over glasses 1 and 2. Second move: Turn over glasses 1 and 3. Third move: Turn over glasses 1 and 2.

"Animal" puzzle (page 51). There are four lions and 31 ostriches. Here's how to figure it out: Since he counted 35 heads, there had to be a minimum of 70 legs. However, his total count of legs was 78, or eight legs more than the minimum. These eight extra legs must, therefore, belong to the lions. Dividing these eight legs by two, we get the number of four-legged animals. Therefore, the total number of lions in the preserve has to be four.

"Horseshoe" puzzle (page 52). Take the second straw in your hand, and with its point, gently raise the horseshoe to a slightly more vertical position so that the upper end of the first straw, the straw that is holding the horseshoe propped up, will fall forward onto the second straw (A). By slightly raising the second straw, you will lock all three items together, and they can be lifted without difficulty (B).

"Mars" puzzle (page 53). Those 50,000 readers who wrote in and said "There is no possible way" were all correct, for that particular sentence is the answer to the puzzle.

"Billiard Ball" puzzle (page 54). The black billiard balls shown in the illustration represent the billiard balls that have to be moved to new positions. The arrows show where they have to be moved to.

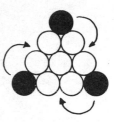

"Crossroads" puzzle (page 55). Napoleon had the pole replaced so that the board that had the name of the town that he had just come from was pointing back down the road he had used to get to the crossroads.

"Pegboard" puzzle (page 56). The illustration shows this magical peg and its bottom, side, and front views.

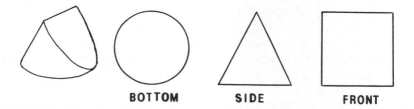

BOTTOM   SIDE   FRONT

"Plate" puzzle (page 57). If you go first, you will always win, providing you place your plate exactly in the middle of the table. Having done that, your opponent will now place his plate somewhere on the table. You, in turn, will now place a plate exactly opposite the spot on the table where he placed his plate. If he places a plate on the northeast corner of the table, you would place your plate on the southwest corner. From this point on, you will always complement his moves in this way. This means that if he can find a spot to place a plate, you will always be able to find a place exactly opposite. When he can't find an open spot, you will be the winner because you placed the last plate on the table.

"Coaster" puzzle (page 58). A to C, on the following page, show how to rearrange the coasters into a perfect circle.

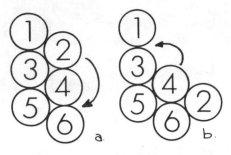
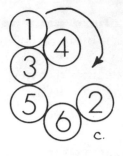

a.   b.   c.

"Tinkertoy" puzzle (page 59). The illustration shows which five rods are removed. When these are removed, five equal triangles are left.

"Cork" puzzle (page 59). Simply fill the glass to the top so that the water is slightly higher than the brim. Gently lower the cork into the water. Since the water forms a "crown" above the rim, the cork will actually float "up" to the middle and stay there.

"Hat" puzzle (page 60). Pick up the chosen hat and place it on your head. No one can deny that the three peanuts are now under the hat.

"Age" puzzle (page 61). Have the person write down her shoe size (forget the ½ sizes). Next, have her multiply the size by 2 and add 5 to the result. Then instruct her to multiply this sum by 50. Now add the "magic number" 1736 to the last product. Finally, have her subtract the year of her birth from the previous sum. Now, ask her what number she is left with. The last two digits of this number will be her age on her birthday this year. (*Note*: Every year, the magic number increases by 1. For example, 1986 = 1736; 1987 = 1737, etc.)

"Record" puzzle (page 62). On *any* record there is just one groove that spirals in towards the middle.

116

"Marble" puzzle (page 63). Once the marble is in the jar, rotate the jar so that the marble is whirling around the sides. Slowly turn the jar upside down. At all times keep the marble whirling in the jar. Centrifugal force will keep the marble from falling out until you place the jar on the table across the room.

"Pyramid" puzzle (page 64). The illustration shows how the pieces can be fitted to form a pyramid.

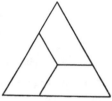

"Circle" puzzle (page 65). Take the square of cardboard and place the tip of one corner against any spot on the inner rim of the circle. Now, at points A and B, where the sides of the cardboard cross the line of the circle, make two marks (see Fig. 1). Using the cardboard as a straightedge, draw a line across the circle from points A and B. Now, placing the tip of the cardboard at some other inner point on the rim of the circle, repeat the actions of step one, placing marks at points C and D (see Fig. 2). Finally, draw a straight line from C to D. The exact center of the circle is where line AB crosses line CD (see Fig. 3).

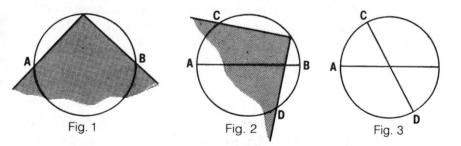

Fig. 1   Fig. 2   Fig. 3

"Dream" puzzle (page 66). Martha knew that since Mr. K— never woke up, no one could possibly know what he had been dreaming about at the time of his death. The story had to be malarkey.

"Postal" puzzle (page 67). The letter was delivered to John Underwood, Andover, England. (That is, JOHN under WOOD and over ENGLAND.)

"Rune Stone" puzzle (page 68). The one thing that all the characters have in common is that they are numbers. Each number, 1 through 9, is chiselled along with its mirror image. If you cover the left half of each figure, you'll see that this is true. The missing number, of course, is six.

"Truck" puzzle (page 69). This would only be true if the driver had an open-bed truck. With an enclosed truck, however, in order for a bird to remain in flight, its wings must push against the air with a force equal to its weight. This causes the air to press down on the bed of the truck with a force equal to the weight of the bird. Thus, the truck will weigh the same whether or not the birds are sitting or flying.

"Betting" puzzle (page 70). Fold the card down the middle, and cut through the line thus made to within a quarter of an inch of each end. The card will then look like Fig. A. Next, with a sharp penknife or scissors, cut through both thicknesses, alternately to right and left, but each time stopping within a quarter of an inch of the edge. See Fig. B. The cuts should be about an eighth of an inch apart. The card when opened will look like Fig. C. Open it out still further and it will form an endless strip, big enough for even J. Wellington Moneybags to step through.

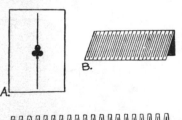

"Bottle" puzzle (page 71). The paper strip is too long to jerk out from under the coins, although this is the method that has to be used to solve this type of problem. What you have to do is cut, or tear, the paper strip off one side about an inch from the stack of coins. Now, take hold of the strip on the other side of the bottle and hold it straight out, 90 degrees from the side of the bottle. With the forefinger of your other hand, strike the paper a sharp blow midway between your hand and the bottle. The paper will be snapped out from under the coins so quickly that inertia will keep them from falling off the bottle top.

"Find-the-Wife" puzzle (page 72). There is no guessing required in this puzzle. It is all a question of elimination. If we can pair off any five of the ladies with their respective husbands, other than husband No. 10, then the remaining lady must be No. 10's wife. I will show how this can be done.

No. 8 is seen carrying a lady's parasol. Every lady is provided with a parasol except No. 3; therefore, No. 3 may be safely said to be the wife of No. 8. No. 12 is holding a bicycle; the dress guard and the make of the bike reveal that it is a lady's bicycle. The only lady in a cycling skirt is No. 5; therefore, we conclude that No. 5 is No. 12's wife. Next, No. 6 has a dog. Therefore, we can safely pair No. 6 with No. 11, who has a dog chain.

No. 2 is paying a newsboy for a paper. However, the gentleman has apparently not taken one from the boy. Lady No. 9 *is* seen reading a paper. The inference is obvious—she has sent her husband to the boy to pay for the newspaper. We therefore pair No. 2 with No. 9.

We have now disposed of all the ladies except Nos. 1 and 7, and of all the men except Nos. 4 and 10. On looking at No. 4, we find that he is carrying a coat over his arm. Since he is already wearing a coat, we can assume that the one he is carrying is a lady's coat, particularly because the buttons are on the left. However, the coat clearly does not belong to No. 1, as she is wearing a coat. No. 7 is very lightly clad. We therefore pair No. 7 with No. 4. Now the only lady left is No. 1; consequently, we are forced to the conclusion that she is the wife of No. 10. This is, therefore, the correct answer.

The illustration on page 72 originally appeared in *The Weekly Dispatch* on May 24, 1903. The original puzzle is by the master of puzzles, Henry Ernest Dudeney.

"X-Ray" puzzle (page 73). Press the paper tightly over the coin. Now, rub a soft-lead pencil over the portion of the paper directly above the coin. An outline, or "rubbing," of the coin will appear showing many features, including the date, quite clearly. You will have certainly proved that you can "see" through solid objects. Why, you could probably even read a date on a silver dollar through aluminum foil. Try this one out.

"Frog" puzzle (page 74). It seems that our frog is ascending at the net rate of one foot a day. At the end of seven days, he's climbed seven feet up the wall. On day eight he climbs the final three feet, which brings him to the top edge of the wall, where, with a final "frogculian" kick, he plops over the rim, tired but happy. The answer, then, is eight days.

"Hotel" puzzle (page 75). The puzzle is deliberately stated in such a manner as to confuse the reader. There is no mysterious disappearing dollar. The lodgers actually paid out $27. Of this, the bellboy took $2 and the hotel received $25. This puzzle is a case of the old verbal "flimflam."

"Pilsner Glass" puzzle (page 76). We will fill the large glass eight times using the small glass. When all the dimensions of a three-dimensional vessel are doubled, its volume is multiplied by a factor of eight. As an example, take a cube 1 foot by 1 foot by 1 foot. Its volume is one cubic foot. Double its dimensions, 2 feet by 2 feet by 2 feet, and you get a volume of eight cubic feet.

"Sea Shell" puzzle (page 77). Since this is a game, there really isn't a solution.

"Policeman" puzzle (page 78). The illustration shows the route the policeman took.

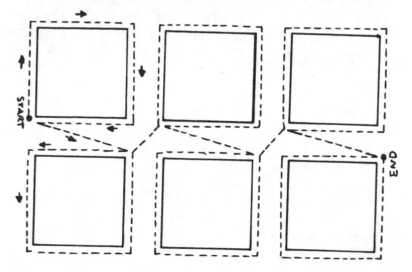

"Lemonade" puzzle (page 79). Judge Fairbench came up with the following solution: Pour four of the half-barrels together. We now have nine full barrels, three half-barrels, and nine empty barrels. All of these can now be evenly divided. Case dismissed!

"Real Estate" puzzle (page 80). George would get nothing for his money. Using the dimensions given, there are zero square feet in the plot. The map drawing is obviously out of proportion to the dimensions. The sides have to be longer than 250 feet or there would be no distance between the 500-foot side and the 1,000-foot side. See the illustration.

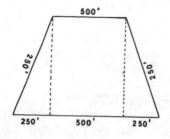

"Crystal" puzzle (page 81). The answer is as clear as crystal. Merely take the glass and gently lower it into the pitcher until it fills with water and sinks to the bottom. The glass will now be filled, yet the pitcher will still contain the same amount of water as before. The next dance is yours!

"Jealous Husband" puzzle (page 82). Let's label the husbands A, B, and C and their wives a, b, and c. The crossing would be made as follows:
1. a and b cross over, and b brings back the boat.
2. b and c cross over, and c returns alone.
3. c lands and remains with her husband, while A and B cross over. A lands and B and b return to the other side.
4. B and C cross over, leaving b and c at the starting point.
5. a takes back the boat and b crosses over with her.
6. a lands and b goes back for c.
7. b and c cross over and all are reunited. Happy ending!

"Bicycle" puzzle (page 83). Betty rode the bike for one hour and covered eight miles. She then left the bike by the side of the road and walked the remaining eight miles, in two hours, to her aunt's house. After walking for two hours, Nadine arrived at the bicycle, and an hour later she pedalled up to the front door of her aunt's house at the same moment Betty arrived. The total time needed to cover the last 16 miles was three hours.

"Testing" puzzle (page 84). The numbers 15 and 16 go into box 3, and number 17 goes into box 2. The numbers in box 1 are all made using curved lines. The numbers in box 2 are made using only straight lines. The numbers in box 3 are made using both straight and curved lines.

"Deductive" puzzle (page 85). What we have to determine is: Does every blue-backed card on the table have a king on its other side? We certainly have to turn over card 1 because it has a blue back. We're not interested in red backed cards, so we'll skip card 2. Number three is a king but it doesn't matter whether its back is blue or red, so we'll skip it too. Finally, we have to turn card 4 over. If card 1 is a king and card 4 is red-backed, the answer is yes. However, if card 1 is not a king, or card 4 has a blue back, then the answer is no.

"Tennis" puzzle (page 86). Since it takes one match to eliminate one couple from play, and we have 128 couples, it would take 127 matches to eliminate all but the winning team.

"Liquid" puzzle (page 87). The answer is simplicity itself. Pick up glass number 2 and pour its contents into glass number 5, and then place glass number 2 back in its original position. The glasses are now alternately filled and empty. Gotcha again!

"Nail" puzzle (page 88). As you can see, in this arrangement each nail touches every other nail.

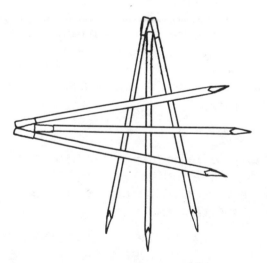

"Knickknack" puzzle (page 89). The illustration on the following page shows you just one of the solutions to the puzzle. Have you figured out any others?

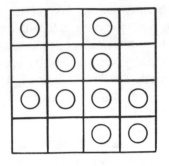

"Travelling" puzzle (page 90). The answer is only *one* was going to St. Ives. Remember, the man telling the story started out by saying, "As I was going to St. Ives . . ." Since he *met* these people, they must have been coming from St. Ives, not going there. If they too had been heading for St. Ives, the man would have *passed* them, or *overtaken* them, but he certainly would not have *met* them.

"Number" puzzle (page 91). Exchange the cards with numbers nine and eight. However, when you place the number nine card in the second column, turn it upside down so that it becomes a six. The numbers in both columns will now add up to 18. I grant you that this is a rather tricky solution, but after all, who promised to play fair 100 percent of the time?

"Antique" puzzle (page 92). The difference between 90 percent of book value and 125 percent of book value is 35 percent. Since 35 percent is worth $105, 1 percent would be worth $3. Therefore, the original book value has to be $300.

"Mr. T" puzzle (page 93). When the leaves are rearranged as shown in the illustration on the following page, "Mr. T" comes to life.

"Fly" puzzle (page 94). Now, most people will decide that the shortest route for our travelling fly to take would be a straight line directly from point A to point D, and then along the edge to point B. Using the Pythagorean Theorem, we calculate that line AD is 2.8284 inches long. (The Pythagorean Theorem states that the length of the longest side of a right triangle is equal to the square root of the sum of the squares of the other two sides of the triangle.)

Now, add to this measurement of 2.8284 inches another 2 inches for line DB and we get a total distance of 4.8284 inches. If, however, we plot a course AC to a point midway along the top edge of the cube, we get a line that is 2.2361 inches long. Also, line CB is 2.2361 inches long. Therefore, we get a total length of 4.4722 inches, a distance considerably shorter than the first "obvious" course.

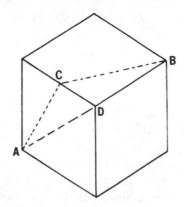

"Marching" puzzle (page 95). Faversham was indeed "having a go" with Maude. The only place on earth that Henry could possibly have made the march described would have been in the Arctic, starting at the North Pole. However, since it wasn't until 1909 that the American explorer Robert Peary first got to the North Pole, I'm afraid Henry will have to forego his place in history.

"Racing" puzzle (page 96). The farmer's solution was for each racer to get into his opponent's buggy. Remember, the original wager specifically stated that "the *first buggy* that crosses the finish line will lose."

"Tire" puzzle (page 97). Since each of the five tires was used for four-fifths of the journey, the answer would be 6,275 miles times 80 percent. This gives us a total of 5,020 miles of wear per tire.

"Brain Teaser" puzzle (page 98). The cards are in the following order: (1) the 2 of clubs, (2) the 3 of clubs, and (3) the 3 of diamonds.

"Candle" puzzle (page 98). If you said four new candles, you're almost right. From 16 candles you get 16 stubs. Divide these by 4 and you get four new candles. But hold on! After you burn these four candles, you will end up with four more stubs from which you can make one more new candle. The correct answer is that Uncle Hay got five extra new candles from every Handy-Pak of 16 candles he bought.

"Cookie" puzzle (page 99). Poor Ariadne started with 15 cookies. Lorella received 7½ + ½, or 8 cookies, leaving 7. Melva received 3½ + ½, or 4 cookies, leaving 3. Laureen received 1½ + ½, or 2 cookies, leaving 1. Finally, Margot was given ½ + ½, or 1 cookie, leaving Ariadne with zilch. Oh, well, there's always next month's mail delivery.

"Archaeology" puzzle (page 100). The errors are as follows: (1) No one in 17 B.C. knew that in 17 years the Christian era would begin with the birth of Christ, so they wouldn't have been counting their years in this fashion; (2) the "C," or *chi*, in the ancient Greek alphabet was drawn like this: "X"; (3) if Pylos's concoction was so powerful, it would have dissolved the amphora as soon as it was poured into it 2,000 years ago.

"Horn" puzzle (page 101). Groucho came up with an ingenious solution. He had the shop wrapper find a large box that measured three feet by four feet. He took the bulb off the horn and packed it into the box on a diagonal from corner to corner. (The length of the diagonal was five feet.) After having the box wrapped up, he now had a package that measured three feet in width by four feet long. The post office had to accept it. The "Case of the Incredible Shrinking Horn" has been solved. See the illustration.

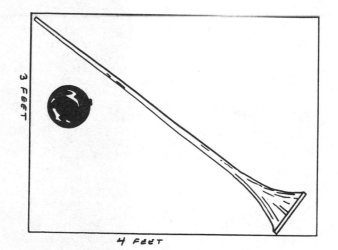

3 FEET

4 FEET

"Wallet" puzzle (page 102). Mr. Gotrocks had one $50 bill, one $5 bill, and four $2 bills.

Index